DOVER
A Pictorial History

St Martin, the patron saint of Dover, as seen on the town's arms, sharing his cloak with a beggar.

DOVER
A Pictorial History

Ivan Green

Phillimore

1987

Published by
PHILLIMORE & CO. LTD.,
SHOPWYKE HALL, CHICHESTER, SUSSEX

ISBN 0 85033 640 6

Printed and bound in Great Britain by
BIDDLES LTD.
Guildford, Surrey

To Margaret

List of Illustrations

Frontispiece: St Martin, patron saint of Dover

1. Pharos and Saxon church, 1850
2. Medieval Dover ship
3. Two 16th-century ships
4. An 18th-century ship
5. The old town plate

Roman and Saxon Dover
6. The Bredenstone in the 18th century
7. The Roman Pharos
8. Roman tile in St Mary in Castro church
9. The Saxon Oval
10. The Saxon church of St Mary in Castro
11. The Saxon south door
12. Harold's Well in the Saxon Oval

Dover Castle
13. Dover Castle from the west, 1735
14. An 18th-century view of Dover Castle from the south-west
15. The Colton Tower and Gate, 1848
16. Dover Castle from the Guston road, 1860
17. View of the Castle by W. Marshall
18. Circular towers of the North Gate
19. The Constable's Tower
20. Napoleonic additions to the defences
21. Modern view of the inner bailey wall and Palace Gate
22. Fore building of the keep
23. Interior view of the keep
24. The second-floor chapel
25. One of the two great state-rooms
26. Storerooms of the castle
27. The great well in the keep

Maison Dieu
28. An 18th-century view of the Maison Dieu
29. The chapel of the Maison Dieu
30. Sale notice for the Maison Dieu, 1834
31. Sale plan for the Maison Dieu
32. A 19th-century view of the Maison Dieu
33. Arched entrance to the Maison Dieu
34. The town hall

Fortifications
35. Archcliffe Fort
36. Site of the old barracks, 1987
37. Gateway to the Citadel
38. The Grand Shaft Barracks
39. The old South Front Barracks
40. Gun turrets on Admiralty Pier

Maps and Plans
41. A 16th-century town map
42. Illustration of the town, 1540
43. Section of the 1595 map showing limekilns
44. Section of the 1595 map showing the Market Square

Historic Buildings
45. The old priory
46. The old priory entrance gate
47. Plan of the inner court of the Priory
48. 'The hole in the wall'
49. The old custom house, c.1806
50. Commercial Quay, c.1840
51. Maison Dieu House, now the public library
52. The original part of the Royal Victoria Hospital
53. Additional wing of the hospital
54. 'Birdcage' public convenience
55. St Edmund's chapel, Priory Street
56. Foundations of the old Knights Templar church
57. The old garrison church
58. Interior of the church of St Mary the Virgin, pre-1843/4
59. Interior of St Mary the Virgin, Easter 1850
60. St Mary's sundial
61. Arms of William and Mary in St Mary's church
62. The west tower of old St Mary the Virgin, Cannon Street
63. Christ Church, Folkestone Road
64. The Roman Catholic church, Maison Dieu Road
65. The Methodist church in Snargate Street, 1965
66. Wesley church, Folkestone Road
67. The Unitarian Chapel
68. The Salem Baptist church, Biggin Street
69. The United Reformed church

Harbour and Docks
70. Harbour entrance, 1796
71. View of the harbour, mid-19th century
72. View of the harbour from the sea, mid-19th century
73. Paddle steamers, 1880
74. View of the Western Docks, 1910
75. Visual communication frame
76. Small 19th-century ships
77. Early steamship, c.1830
78. Later paddle steamers, c.1900
79. King George V's yacht, *Britannia*
80. Submarines in Dover harbour between the wars
81. Print of Yorrick and his wife, 1775
82. Passengers landing at Admiralty Pier
83. Arrival of the steam packet, 1860
84. A modern arrival
85. Crane loading coach onto car ferry
86. View of the Car Ferry Docks
87. Christmas Day in the Western Docks
88. The Wellington Dock
89. The harbour from the Western Heights
90. The breakwater

Promenade and Pier
91. The pier district, 1735
92. Marine Parade, c.1820
93. Early 20th-century view of the promenade
94. The promenade pier
95. Pier company share certificate
96. Concert hall on Dover pier

Shops, Businesses and Public Services
97. Advertisement for tailors and outfitters
98. William Eastes, corn merchants
99. Advertisement for Walter Day Adams, wine and spirit merchants
100. Advertisement for Major Munn's bar frame hive
101. Ingram Newman, specialist in shell fish
102. 'The Crystal'
103. Lukey and Sons, wine merchant
104. London Outfitters Ltd.
105. The end of Woolworths, 1984
106. The tiny window in the gable end of the *Elephant and Hind*
107. Restaurant above Igglesden and Graves's baker's shop
108. Igglesden Corner in Market Square
109. The Connaught Park waterworks
110. A triple-expansion vertical steam engine
111. A Cornish-type boiler
112. Waterwork's well
113. Oil engine which powered the sewage pumps

Inns and Hotels
114. The old *City of Antwerp Hotel*
115. Tariff of charges for the *Burlington Hotel*
116. External view of the *Burlington Hotel*
117. The hotel lounge
118. The shell of the *Burlington*
119. Ruins of the *Burlington Hotel*
120. The old *Cause is Altered*
121. The *Hotel de France*
122. The *Prince Regent* and Market Hall
123. The *Sir John Falstaff* Inn
124. The *Dover Stage*
125. The *White Cliffs Hotel*

Transport
126. The turnpike gate on the Dover-Deal-Sandwich road
127. Site of the turnpike gate on the Folkestone-Dover road
128. Experimental work on the Channel Tunnel, 1880
129. Invitation to the opening of the Dover to Deal Railway, 1881
130. Terminus of the London, Chatham and Dover Railway
131. Early train at Aycliffe
132. The early S.E.R. terminus on the beach
133. The Marine Station
134. Arthur Baldock on 'King of the Road'
135. Steam traction engine
136. Horse-drawn wagons and open-top tram, c.1910
137. Railway and tram services outside Holy Trinity church, 1932
138. First tram on its maiden run to River, 1905
139. An open-top tram

Demolition and Damage
140. Demolition of the Antwerp Stables
141. The end of old Worthington Lane, 1895
142. The last days of Beach Street
143. Clearance of Beach Street, 1975
144. The old houses in Albany Place
145. The old Gorely Homes
146. The war-damaged Hippodrome
147. The wreckage of Chitty's flour mill
148. War damage in the seafront area
149. The Gateway Flats
150. Old St James's church before clearance
151. Old St James's today

Special Occasions
152. A colours ceremony, c.1860
153. Prince of Wales laying foundation stone of new harbour, 1893
154. A French concert in the Maison Dieu Hall, 1855

155. 'Inauguration' of the town hall organ
156. Parade along the seafront
157. Leney Brewery decorated for the Lord Warden's visit
158. Regatta day, 1924
159. Bandstand in the Granville Gardens, c.1910
160. The last church parade of the old Borough Council, 1974
161. H.R.H. Queen Elizabeth, the Queen Mother, inspecting the naval guard of honour, 1979
162. The great pageant of 1909
163. Participants in the 1986 pageant

Acknowledgements

The writer of any book is of necessity indebted to many people who have given advice, information, support and encouragement. I should like to express my grateful thanks to all who have helped me, and especially to Mrs. Frances Mee of Phillimore & Co., the staff of the Kent County Libraries and the Dover Museum, to Mrs. Sylvia Corrall, Miss Christine Waterman, Mrs. Mary Stevens, Mr. Ron Chatburn, Dr. Richard Stevens, Mr. Ray Warner, and to three members of English Heritage in Dover, Mr. Ken Scott, Mr. John Sutton, and in particular to Mr. Stephen Carswell who knows and loves his castle so well.

Though most of the material used in this book is taken from his own collection, the author would like to thank a number of people who have lent him photographs, drawings and prints over the past years to be copied for publication: the late Mr. T. D. Crellin, nos. 37, 38 and 39; the Dover branch of the Kent County Library service, nos. 28, 29, 31, 41, 54, 158 and 159; Mrs. P. Newman, no. 101; the late Mr. John Sutton, nos. 47, 72, 80, 82, 83 and 153. He has also photographed the castle and defence works by kind permission of English Heritage, and local authority installations by kind permission of Dover District Council. He wishes to express his grateful thanks to them all and to anyone inadvertently omitted.

Historical Introduction

In prehistoric times Dover was a tiny inland settlement beside the freshwater stream, now called the Dour, which flowed down a a deep cleft in the great chalk hills between Walmer and Sandgate. It became a coastal village approximately seven or eight thousand years ago when the waters of the English Channel broke through the neck of land which had joined England to the continent. From that time onwards the beaches of south-east Kent provided landing places for Neolithic, Bronze Age and Iron Age men who had crossed the Channel in their dugout boats and crude rafts. No doubt many of them sailed into the little harbour formed by the river Dour flowing into the sea.

Neolithic men left behind their stone tools and Bronze Age men left fine gold torques, such as those discovered on the valley floor in 1772 and 1878. Iron Age men built a number of hill forts across the county, including a large one on Dover's eastern heights which was the ancient forerunner of the present castle. According to the Kent historians Abell and Jessup, the Belgae arrived from Gaul in increasing numbers from about 100 B.C. and strengthened the hill forts against the threat of a Roman invasion.

Their efforts were in vain, however, and after a second landing of the legions in 54 B.C. the Romans withdrew leaving, according to an old tradition, a British puppet king named Mandubratius, who established a praetorium within the old Iron Age fort at *Dubris*, the Roman name for Dover. The full-scale assault of the legions occurred in A.D. 43 and from that time Britain became part of the great Roman empire. *Dubris*, being one of the few deep water anchorages in east Kent, was developed both as a port and as a base for the *Classis Britannica*, the Roman fleet. Like most important ports in the Roman Empire, the entrance to Dover from the sea was marked by two great beacons on the eastern and western heights. That on the eastern heights, within the bounds of the old Iron Age fort and the present castle, now called the Pharos, survives as one of the most complete Roman buildings remaining in Britain. The one on the western heights, called the Bredenstone, has sadly almost disappeared, only a few pieces of masonry surviving.

Roman remains have been discovered all over the valley, but all traces of the actual town of *Dubris* seemed to have been lost until 1971 when major excavations, prior to the redevelopment of war-damaged property to the west of Market Square, were carried out by the C.I.B. (Kent) Archaeological Corps led by Mr. Brian Philp. The results were dramatic. The foundations and much of the walls of a great fort were discovered together with the now famous painted house. A further discovery was a later great defensive work, a Saxon shore fort, which covered part of the older fort of the *Classis Britannica*. The town may have been deserted by the Roman fleet because the harbour was silting up and the later fort was built as a defensive measure against the increasing number of raids by Saxon ships from the third century onwards.

Dubris was the starting point of several Roman roads. Sections of those to Canterbury and Richborough have survived, but all trace of a third road linking Dover with Folkestone and Lympne seems to have been lost.

1. A fine old drawing of the Roman Pharos and the Saxon church published by the Dover printer, Thomas Rigden, in 1850.

With the collapse of the authority of the Empire, raids from tribesmen of north-west Europe became more frequent and devastating, and few records of Dover's history have survived from these centuries. It would have been dangerous to live in the valley, round the river, the old docks and the decaying Roman forts, so most people probably lived on the eastern heights within the perimeter of the old fort. It may have been there that King Eadbald established his college of secular priests or canons in A.D. 620. According to the *Victoria County History of Kent*, King Wihtred moved them down to a new site on the old Roman remains to the west of the Market Place in A.D. 696. There is no conclusive evidence of this, but if it did happen it would prove that seaborne raids were becoming fewer by that time.

A little over a century later a new menace threatened Dover, since from about 830 repeated Danish raids brought more disaster to Kent. It is probable that from this time Dover became a burgh or borough. In return for the privilege of self government, the right to fish the seas and trade with the continent and, from the reign of Edward the Elder (899-924) at least, for its own mint, the town became responsible for its own defence.

A much clearer picture of the later Saxon town emerges from various records and from Domesday Book in particular. There was a settlement to the west of the Market Square which probably contained the guildhall, a small group of houses at Warden Down, the land under the cliff between old St James's church and the sea, and the old borough on the site of the Iron Age fort on Castle Hill. The Saxon church of St Mary in Castro, one of the finest surviving pre-Conquest churches in the country, indicates that there was a good-sized community on Castle Hill.

Dover was a large and prosperous town with many ships and mariners – it provided the king with 20 ships, each manned by 20 men, for 15 days every year at its own cost, and for a further 15 days, if required, at the king's cost. There was considerable trade in goods between Dover and the continent and Dover ships provided a cross-channel service for kings, emperors, ministers of church and state, traders, and later pilgrims. The town at this time was ruled by a praepositor (later to become the mayor), a reeve and burgesses, who met in their own guildhall. The burgesses owned property, some a single house, others several – William Godfrey, the praepositor, owned two houses and the town's guildhall.

Disaster struck when William of Normandy, having won the Battle of Hastings, marched east to invade Dover, no doubt recognising its strategic significance. Dover resisted for some days and this enraged him. He had Bertram Ashburnham and his son beheaded at the gate of the borough on top of the hill, and expelled all the civilian population. William's troops were completely out of hand and set about the townsfolk in the valley, committing robbery, rape and murder, and burning the wooden houses to the ground. However, William needed Dover and its ships, which controlled his lifeline to Normandy. It was therefore essential that he should pacify the people of the town, so he confirmed all their earlier privileges, including their right to self government. A great building programme was initiated and this, continuing through the end of the 11th, the 12th and the early 13th centuries, created in effect a new town.

The principal new buildings in the town itself were the imposing church of the old secular canons, known as St Martin le Grand, built on land covering the old Roman forts; the church of St Peter in the Market Square; St Mary the Virgin, which grew from a tiny two-cell building to almost its present size; old St James's; and a small hospice for travellers which developed into a large and imposing building, part of which is now the town hall. The secular canons of old St Martin le Grand had long been a thorn in the flesh of the medieval church and its archbishops who had no authority over them and coveted their possessions and land. Archbishop Corbeil blackmailed King Henry I into permitting the establishment of a monastery for regular canons outside the town, and the transfer of all the property and income of the venerable old institution to the new foundation. Thus, at the stroke of a pen, the ancient institution was dissolved and its canons dispersed. The great new monastery was built very rapidly and was known as St Martin of the New Wark, though it was later referred to as Dover Priory. The 400 years of its history were neatly summed up by Charles Reginald Haines, author of *Dover Priory* which was published in 1930, as 200 years of constant quarrelling with the monks of Christ Church Canterbury, followed by 200 years of subservience to them. Several surviving buildings then became a farm for a further 300 years until, in the 19th century, the site was used for the building of Dover College.

By far the greatest building operation was the conversion of the old fort on the eastern heights, until then simply earthen banks surmouted by wooden palisading, into the great stone castle we know today. Henry II was largely responsible for this work from 1168 onwards. The great keep and the inner and outer bailey walls were built in the years after 1180. All the work was supervised by two great master masons, Master Ralph and Maurice the Engineer. Some of the building was incomplete when Henry II died and expenditure on the castle continued into the reign of Richard I. His successor, John, faced the threat of invasion from France, exacerbated by the disloyalty of many of his own barons, so, after the English lost Normandy in 1204, he spent large sums on the outer walls and gates of Dover Castle. The work was completed not a moment too soon. Some of the dissident barons invited Louis, son of the French king, to bring over an army to depose John and take the English crown. There was a full-scale raid on Kent in which Canterbury and much of its hinterland was occupied by the invaders who then settled down to conduct a siege of the newly-completed castle at Dover.

In spite of the efforts of the French, using the latest rock-throwing siege engines, the captain of the tiny defence force within, the legendary Hubert de Burgh, refused to submit, though his body of men became progressively smaller as casualties mounted. Just in time, he received reinforcements from Stephen de Pencestre who smuggled his 400 men into the castle through a secret passage at the north of the outer walls. The French then resorted to mining and their tunnel towards the great north gate brought down its eastern flanking tower, leaving a huge gaping hole which the defenders managed to plug from inside. At last King John died and the invaders returned to France, having failed completely in their campaign.

Henry III inherited a country in turmoil and Dover Castle in a severely damaged state, so that over the next few years major work had to be undertaken. It was obvious that the great north gate, with high ground outside it, was a source of weakness and so it was blocked up. The damaged east flanking tower was rebuilt and, besides earthworks, St John's tower was built outside the old gate. To give access to the castle a small opening in the outer wall was converted into the impressive entrance now known as the Constable's Tower and this, consisting of no less than five towers built close together, is still standing today. The strengthening of the outer perimeter walls towards the edge of the cliff completed the major works so that the castle today is essentially as it was in the middle of the 13th century, though of course some modifications were made later.

These centuries were not monopolised totally by great building operations. They were the heyday of the Cinque Ports. Time and again Dover seamen joined the Cinque Port fleet in sea battles, starting with the complete defeat of a Danish raiding fleet in the straits in 1069. The Scottish expedition of 1091 resulted in the loss of many ships and their crews, but Dover mariners played a major role in the crusading fleet which captured Lisbon from the Moors in 1147 and in transporting Richard I's crusading army in 1190. Such events, however, were occasional. The Dover men in their little ships continued their service to the Crown year by year, repelling seaborne invaders, transporting kings and their armies to France, and working the Passage so that cross-channel governmental and cultural contacts could be maintained and trade increased.

Life in the 13th century became much more violent for the people of Dover. After King John lost Normandy the straits ceased to be an Anglo-Norman bridge between two associated lands and became instead a barrier between two hostile nations. Dover, as one of the Cinque Ports, was repeatedly required to supply its quota of ships to the Crown, over and above its contracted number of days. They were involved in a great victory in 1213 at the Battle of Damme when hundreds of French ships were sunk and over 200 captured. The Portsmen were wild and undisciplined, and between their more official engagements they were frequently in disgrace for their own unauthorised raids on continental coastal towns and ports, piracy on the high seas and wrecking, all of which became endemic.

2. This early Dover Cinque Ports ship, shown on an old Dover coat of arms, is typical of the 12th and 13th centuries. It had a planked hull, a single central mast supporting a square sail and was propelled by oars. Here it is shown fitted up with great boxes, called castles, ready to render its ship service to the Crown. The three boxes contained the fighting men and were, respectively, the fore castle, the stern castle and the mast head castle. Ships today still have forecastles.

Dover, with the other ports, supported Simon de Montfort in the Barons' War of 1258-65 but 1282 saw them fighting with the king's forces in the Welsh campaign, losing many of their ships and men in the capture of Anglesey. They seem to have recovered well since a full complement of Dover ships and men were engaged in the Scottish campaign in 1290.

There were, of course, years of peace and tranquility even in those troubled times. Dover fishermen landed large quantities of fish, especially herrings, most of which were dried, salted and packed in barrels for sale to religious communities, in south-east England and on the continent. Ships continued to be built on Dover beach, strong and lithe ships, the envy of sailors everywhere. At coronations selected Dover men went to London to join other Portsmen who carried the canopy over the king during the procession and sat on his right hand at the coronation feast. Most important of all, every Dovorian was born free at a time when free men were rare. The domination of secular governments, and the threats of medieval barons and greedy princes of the church were all kept at bay by the town's treasured royal charters.

As the 13th century progressed the little ships of the Cinque Ports became less important as larger ships from ports with deeper harbours were used more frequently for royal service. At the same time the French were becoming a major threat with their more numerous and larger ships and improved standards of seamanship. The French took advantage of the absence of the Dover ships engaged under the king in Scottish wars in 1295 to raid a number of Kent coastal towns including Dover. Their 500 ships and 30 galleys were a formidable force and, when they put ashore a landing party, they found the town undefended, most able-bodied men being away in Scotland. Many people fled, but the French burnt many buildings and massacred all those unable to escape. One raiding party made its way straight to the Priory, burning the gates and systematically ransacking every building. Most monks ran away to hide, but old Thomas de la Hale confronted the French as they looted the precious belongings of the Priory and refused to show them where his own treasure was hidden. Unable to move him, they murdered him in his own dormitory and returned to their ships. Meanwhile those citizens who had escaped came back to the town with reinforcements and drove the raiders out, inflicting heavy losses on them according to the old chronicles. Nevertheless, Dover had lost many of its older citizens, many houses and those ships which had not been away in Scotland. Years afterwards there was a great campaign to get Thomas de la Hale canonised, but the monks of Canterbury were determined not to allow a saint in Dover as a rival to their own St Thomas, source of considerable wealth to the cathedral town.

There were from time to time scenes of pageantry and colour such as the arrival of Edward II in Dover in 1308, with many of his courtiers all brightly attired. He sailed from Dover to France to marry Isabella, a French princess. Such days must have enlivened the rather dull existence of many, in particular the women who never travelled far from their homes.

But the French were becoming more of a threat all the time and their larger ships were gaining superiority over the small craft of the Portsmen. The second half of the 14th century witnessed the enclosure of Dover within a protective stone wall, broken by gates at strategic points. Work seems to have started in 1368 and was complete by 1384. In 1372/3 £76 19s. 8d. was paid out for materials and labour – there seem to have been 10 men working on the walls at wages of 6d. each per day, the materials being bought as they were needed. One typical account reads: '25 quarters of lime delivered to the site 3s. 0d., 4 cartloads of stone 1s. 6d. with 3d. extra for carriage and £3 5s. 0d. for wood, tiles etc. for roofing in the wall gate'. The money was raised by means of a cess, a forerunner of the present rates system, and when the money was spent a new cess was ordered. This construction of a town wall was a tacit admission of the increasing strength of the continental enemy, and of Dover's inability to defend itself from raiding parties or to respond in kind.

The Portsmen's ships continued to be involved in national campaigns. Dover ships served in the great Battle of the Sluys in 1340 and helped transport armies across the Channel, for example to the Battle of Crecy in 1346 and Agincourt in 1415. After returning from Agincourt, Henry V headed a victory procession through the streets of Dover. Royal returns were not always triumphal however. In 1422 Henry V died in France and his body was brought home in a Dover ship. The sad procession escorting the coffin, draped in a great black pall, wound its way through the town in mournful silence.

When Henry VIII came to Dover, as he so often did, the town was in a very poor condition. The old harbour was silting up, restricting the Passage trade and fishing – ships now had to be launched from the open beach and even this was only possible in good conditions. Demand for fish had dropped as many of the old religious institutions which had been good customers were themselves in decline. The great age of faith was already over.

Dover's once great Priory was now practically insolvent. There were too few members even to say the Passage Mass regularly, the two or three novices were receiving no instruction and the buildings were in a state of decay. The Maison Dieu, that once important hospice for travellers and pilgrims, was in a similar condition, and old St Martin le Grand on the west side of the Market Square, with its three parish altars under one roof, had passed beyond the possibility of repair even if sufficient money had been available for the task. Large numbers of citizens, if not actively hostile to the religious and their institutions, were quite indifferent to the threat to their survival. Dover's religious houses were dissolved in the 1530s and the monks of Dover Priory were pensioned off. Most of the buildings, including the great church, were demolished and the materials sold, the profits finding their way for the most part into private pockets. The leper hospital on Chapel Hill was granted to a Dover man for his lifetime – he razed all the buildings to the ground. Old St Martin le Grand became a ruin and the corporation assumed control of much of it, but the Maison Dieu continued to cater for a few travellers for several years after the dissolution. The church of St Peter, on the north side of the Market Square where Lloyds Bank now stands, was appropriated by the corporation for use as its official church. Henry VIII, in response to the people's request, gave them the church of St Mary the Virgin, free of all cost, as their own parish church.

Henry, having offended the Pope, France and Spain, was in need of improved defences to guard against the threat of invasion, so he built castles and gun platforms all round the coast of south-east England. In Dover, where there was already a strong castle, he built three small forts for guns to cover the beach and its approaches. Mote's Bulwark, in the cliff below the castle, and part of Archcliffe Fort, at the west end of the sea front, still survive, although much altered in Napoleonic times. The site of Henry VIII's old Black Battery has been covered by the Western Dock developments. Henry listened to appeals from the men of Dover for improvements to the harbour and he supplied money for the work to be done. A great breakwater was built, but ships continued to work in difficult conditions. He made a number of ceremonial visits to the town, the most notable being his departure on 31 May 1520, with his splendid entourage, to meet the King of France at the Field of the Cloth of Gold.

The people of Dover revered Elizabeth I who visited the town on two occasions. To her they owed their much-prized charter and the pent, an artificial harbour which is now part of the Western Docks complex. During her reign, in 1588, the Spanish Armada sailed into the English Channel. By this time the Cinque Port ships had largely been displaced by larger ships fighting a completely different kind of sea warfare. However, Dover supplied the *Elizabeth*, a ship of 120 tons with a crew of 70 and provisions for 50 days, as well as some smaller vessels. These ships saw action near Gravelines under the command of Admiral Seymour.

Haines maintains that in 1565 there were 358 houses in Dover, 20 ships and crayers, 120 vessels of about four tons, and 130 people employed in trade or

3. Here are two naval ships of the 16th century at Dover, photographed from the map drawing of the 1540s.

shipping. These would have been men in positions of authority, as ships' crews, fishermen, craftsmen and general shore workers would not have been included.

The people of Dover had little for which to be grateful to the Stuarts and, from the accession of James I in 1603 to the flight of James II in 1688, the town faced troubled times. In 1606 James I removed control of the harbour from the townsfolk and granted it to 'eleven discreet men', consisting of the Lord Warden, the Lieutenant of Dover Castle, the Mayor, and eight knights and squires. It is unlikely that any of them were knowledgeable about the maintenance and running of a harbour. Charles I came to Dover in 1625 to meet his bride, Henrietta Maria, when she arrived from France and he also spent £2,600 on the royal apartments in the castle, but nothing on the defences. These were almost in ruins, and during the Civil War the castle, held by only a handful of troops, was stormed by a citizen of Dover named Vaux and 10 associates who handed it over to the parliamentary forces with whom it remained until the Restoration.

Charles II was brought back from exile on the continent to take the crown in 1660 by a convoy of ships including the *Naseby* under the command of Captain William Stokes, a Dover man who later played an important part in the town's history. On arriving at Dover, the king was ferried ashore in a small boat because the harbour was choked with shingle, an event well documented by Samuel Pepys who accompanied him. Charles II was no friend to Dover and the people had to pay very dearly for their support of Parliament during the Civil War and the Commonwealth. He replaced the treasured Elizabethan charter with one of his own and repeatedly interfered with the town's choice of leaders and its civic decisions. Time and again mayors and councillors were thrown out of office, religious persecution especially of the Dissenters was rife, and anyone even suspected of disloyalty was severely punished. The year 1665 saw the outbreak of the great plague. It killed more than 900 people in Dover and many others never fully recovered. The dead were hastily buried in communal pits to the west of the town and this area, called 'the Graves', remains deserted and undeveloped to this day.

Charles II came to the castle and held a great court assembly there to entertain the French king on the occasion of the signing of the secret treaty in 1670, his last visit to the town. His brother, later James II, was appointed Lord Warden of the Cinque Ports and Governor of Dover Castle, and was officially installed at the Bredenstone, the old Roman beacon on the Western Heights, in 1688. Four years later he met his bride, the 15-year old Princess Mary of Modena, when she arrived in Dover from the continent. When James II fled abroad in 1689 the people of the town were summoned to the Market Square by a horn to hear the news of his departure. The official celebration continued for days, as the four Stuart kings had brought little but trouble and disaster to Dover.

One might describe the first half of the 18th century as the lull before the storm of change which was to usher in a new and strange world. Continuing problems with the harbour produced a number of minor works, not all successful. The Passage ships and those of the now well established Dover export and import traders prospered in the main and developed into fast, responsive and seaworthy vessels, built on Dover beach and able to cross to France in a single tide.

Ashore, the old town was a maze of narrow streets, lanes and winding secret alleys. All kinds of houses, large and small, jostled for room among stables, cow byres and pig styes, a brewery, inns and tanneries, besides small workshops where craftsmen made and sold their wares. The roads were covered in gravel and mud and a central drainage ditch overflowed with general refuse, offal and the droppings of horses whose hooves constantly stirred up the fetid contents. Sewage simply drained into the river or harbour, and the drinking water of the inhabitants was drawn from numerous wells which were often polluted with sewage. Disease was endemic and house fires were frequent and sometimes disastrous. Strangers, whether fellow countrymen or foreigners, were not welcomed into this close knit community. They were actively discouraged and not allowed to set up in business or even seek employment, other than in exceptional circumstances.

Then from the middle of the 18th century a succession of events swept away the old order and introduced two centuries of constant change. Travel increased dramatically after the building of the turnpike roads. The Dover to Folkestone, and the Dover to Barham roads became turnpikes in 1753, that to Deal and Sandwich in 1797, and those to Whitfield, Eastry and Sandwich, and the connecting link up Whitfield Hill between Kearsney and Whitfield, were completed in 1801. There was naturally then an increase in horse-drawn coaches and service coaches, not only to London but also to principal towns all over the county. Shipping services and trade, in spite of recurrent wars, expanded too.

Defence was also greatly improved and modernised. A detailed inspection was made of the castle by the Duke of Cumberland in the mid-18th century and,

4. An 18th-century ship in Dover bay.

following this, many repairs were undertaken and accommodation provided for 1,000 troops. In 1779, when England was at war with France, Spain and the American colonies, the Guildford Battery was built at the foot of the castle cliff and three earthen batteries on the sea front, besides two overlooking the bay in the castle grounds. It was at this time that the appearance of the old castle was fundamentally changed. Old towers, walls, battlements and buildings were destroyed to provide gun positions with unobstructed firing arcs. Saddest of all was the destruction of the upper part of the great keep and the installation there of the great brick vaults. Earthworks and gun positions were erected on the Western Heights in 1779 and were later made permanent in great engineering works which continued into the early years of the 19th century.

In the town itself the period was marked by great social changes. The garrisoning of thousands of soldiers in and around the town caused a major distortion of the old exclusive Dovorian society – this is well documented in the birth and marriage registers. Dover's first Local Government Acts of 1778, 1810, 1830 and 1835 provided for the improvement and lighting of the streets, the institution of watchers to guard the town, and control of many local activities including bathing.

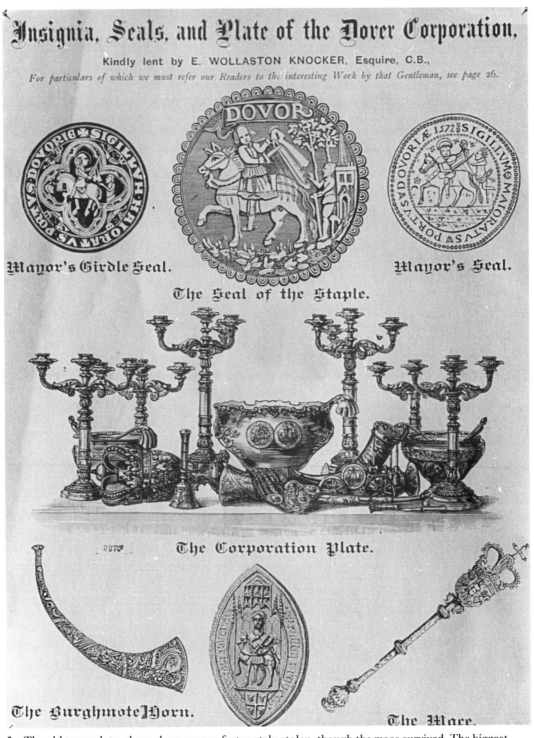

Insignia, Seals, and Plate of the Dover Corporation,

Kindly lent by E. WOLLASTON KNOCKER, Esquire, C.B.,

For particulars of which we must refer our Readers to the interesting Work by that Gentleman, see page 26.

Mayor's Girdle Seal.

The Seal of the Staple.

Mayor's Seal.

The Corporation Plate.

The Burghmote Horn.

The Mace.

5. The old town plate, shown here, was unfortunately stolen, though the mace survived. The biggest loss was the old Burghmote Horn which, being centuries old, was irreplaceable.

The long years of military threats from the continent ended with England's victory at sea in the Battle of Trafalgar in 1805 and on land at Waterloo in 1815. From that time, Dover's progress into modern times was rapid.

The first steam packet, the *Rob Roy*, began to ply the Passage in 1820 and soon steam was challenging sail, though both passengers and goods had to rely on horse-drawn travel to and from the port until the opening of the Dover terminus of the South-Eastern Railway in 1844, and that of the London, Chatham and Dover in 1860. The effect on the town was dramatic. The horse-drawn stage coach services dwindled and died. Hundreds of men lost their jobs. Unemployment was aggravated by the decline in the building of wooden sailing ships which were being replaced by steamships, and the compulsory purchase of the Archcliff Beach Shipyards to provide land for the S.E.R. line from Folkestone to the Western Docks.

The middle of the 19th century brought a flurry of military activity because of a new French invasion threat. Great defence works on the Western Heights, including the building of extra defence positions and the garrison church, were carried out. It was at this time that the foundations of the old circular church at Braddon, hidden by earlier military building, were again exposed to view, and the remains of the old Bredenstone were also revealed again.

Work continued on the harbour, but Dover mariners were still not satisfied and blamed the inadequacy on the country squires who were the harbour commissioners. The Parliamentary Inquiry of 1836 eventually bore fruit since, besides recommending major modifications to the harbour, it also led to the formation of the Harbour Board in 1861 which still continues to control and develop harbour facilities. The 19th century also saw the development of the sea front. The great shingle bank which had been built up by sea and tide and had for centuries been the town's ropewalk, was built on. Marine Parade was erected in 1820, work on the Esplanade was begun in 1833 and Waterloo Crescent, which survived the last war, in 1834. Thus the sea front was lined with smart new houses and for some years formed desirable accommodation for 'the better and more select kind of professional people's holidays'. At this time there was also a movement to try to make the town a popular middle class holiday resort for people to whom Brighton or Margate 'and such similar vulgar retreats would be socially impossible'. However Dover has always been, and remains, more of a commercial than a tourist centre.

The 20th century is as yet too young to permit a historical perspective, but some important events must at least be mentioned. The completion of the great Admiralty harbour, by lengthening the Admiralty pier and building the eastern arm and the breakwater, provided a great new naval base which, because of the development of long-range guns capable of firing across the Channel, submarines, torpedoes and aeroplanes, was largely useless for its original purpose. It has, however, given the town a magnificent enclosed harbour.

Two great wars, the second causing terrible damage to the town through the action of enemy guns and aerial bombing, destroyed much of the old town, and have probably also witnessed the end for the area as the front line of the country's defences and of its strategic importance as a military garrison. Dover's future must be non-military for the first time. But Dover is still the Port of the Passage and the development of the Western Docks, though important, has been rather over-shadowed by the remarkable success of the roll on-roll off car ferry docks at the Eastern Arm which are continually being improved and extended to keep pace with the ever increasing private and commercial traffic it serves so well. Today great new ships, hovercrafts and jetfoils cross the Channel where earlier generations of men ventured on their crude rafts and in their dugout boats and where the ships of the Roman *Classis Britannica* once dominated the narrow sea. Dover's long and distinguished seafaring tradition is now perhaps threatened by modern aircraft or by the revival of ancient, mole-like burrowings under the sea, but it will almost certainly not be destroyed.

It is of course quite impossible to deal in any adequate way with Dover's long history in a few thousand words, and this brief summary can only be considered as a series of lamps or signposts on a very long journey, very much in the tradition of a very good pen-friend who, arriving from overseas several years ago, 'did' Britain and Europe in a fortnight!

Roman and Saxon Dover

6. The Bredenstone as it was in the 18th century. It was the second of the two Roman beacons indicating the entrance to Dover harbour. The few surviving remains are on the top of the Drop Redoubt.

7. (*left*) The Roman Pharos in Dover Castle grounds, the companion beacon to Bredenstone, and said to be one of the most complete Roman buildings left in the country. The top is medieval; at one time it was used as a bell tower to the church nearby.

8. (*right*) This Roman tile in St Mary in Castro church bears the marks of seagull feet and, at the centre, the spoor of a Siberian wolf, impressions made on the surface when the tile was drying.

9. The great earthwork surrounding the church and Pharos was part of the early earthen defences and is known as the Saxon Oval.

10. The Saxon church of St Mary in Castro. Though much repaired in the 19th century by Scott and Butterfield, it remains one of the finest Saxon churches in the country.

11. (*left*) Canon Puckle's drawing of the Saxon south door when it was first uncovered. The Saxon 'long and short' work is beautifully shown. This was used in his report on St Mary in Castro in the 19th century.

12. (*below*) Harold's Well in the Saxon Oval. It is thought to have been dug by Harold to fulfil the promise he made to William of Normandy that, as well as resigning the crown of England to him if he inherited it from Edward the Confessor, he would strengthen the defences of Dover Castle and dig a well of sweet water there.

Dover Castle

To the most Noble LIONEL, Duke & Earl of Dorset Earl of Middlesex Baron Buckhurst
aron Cranfield of Cranfield Lord Lieut.t of Ireland. Lord Warden of the Cinque Ports
stable of Dover Castle Custos Rotulorum for the County of Kent One of the Lords of his
ESTIES most Hon.ble Privy Council & Knight of the most Noble Order of the Garter
This Prospect is with all Humility Inscrib'd by
his Graces most humbly Devoted & most Faithful Serv.t
Sam.l & Nath.l Buck

The Town of Dover is remarkable for its Antiquity, and The Notitia of y.e Western Empire confirms
by allowing y.e Romans to have had a Garrison here. To commemorate is y.e Harbour y.e Julius Cæsar in his first
Expedition to Conquer Britain had a design to land here. This Castle an Antient Building is mounted above y.e Town
both to command & defend it. But y.e Conqueror took it A.D.1060. On K. Stephen Queen besieging it y.e Governor surr-
der'd A.D.1036 K. Hen.II built y.e high Tower. The Castle A.D.1258 was deliver'd up to Philip Earl of Flanders
but after his departure K. Hen.III granted this place to Hubert de Burgh Earl of Kent.

13. The S. and N. Buck drawing of Dover Castle from the west in 1735. These artists produced and published many **fine** drawings at that time, their detail work being especially fine. This was one of the last drawings of the castle before **the** major Napoleonic modifications.

14. Dover Castle from the south-west in the first half of the 18th century, engraved and published as part of a series by Newman and Barclay, but not dated.

15. The Colton Tower and Gate of the castle, 'Published by Thomas Rigden 28th. August 1848 and sold by all booksellers'. This Thomas Rigden published many fine illustrations of Dover.

16. Dover Castle from the Guston road in 1860. The house just to the left of centre is the tollgate keeper's house.

17. This view was published by W. Marshall, No. 1. Holborn Bars, in the second half of the 18th century. It shows old walls in the foreground, which have since been demolished.

18. The two circular towers of the old North Gate of the castle survive, though the left (eastern) one was rebuilt **solid** after the 1216 siege. Note that it has no arrow slits. The central pointed beak of stone fills the space once occupied by the main entrance door.

19. The outer walls of the castle, looking from the blocked north gate to the post-1216 entrance known as the Constable's Tower.

20. In Napoleonic days further additions, of which these were a part, were made to the defences outside the old blocked North Gate, to allow flanking fire to be directed against enemy troops besieging the walls.

21. The inner bailey wall and the Palace Gate as it is today. The square towers were obsolete after the first decade of the 13th century, when round towers came into general use. The great square keep behind was the work of the king's master mason, Maurice the Engineer. He came straight to Dover from Newcastle, where his castle gave the town its name.

22. (*left*) The fore building of the keep was erected to make entry to it as difficult as possible for an enemy. Here, at the top of the first flight of steps, one entered and then had to turn sharp left. This photograph also shows the battering or outward slope of the keep walls. This inhibited the use of a battering ram by an enemy besieging the keep, and also spread the enormous weight of the stone walls over a greater area of foundations.

23. (*right*) Once inside the keep, one was confronted by more stairs, then a moveable bridge over a deep pit, more stairs and then a guardroom, before having to turn sharp left to enter the interior proper. This fore building was originally roofless and open to the sky, only being roofed in later centuries.

24. The second-floor chapel as it was until recently. Being built into the corner tower of the keep, it was of course never roofless and its Norman carving remains fresh and undamaged. Unfortunately it is now shut off by an unsightly metal grill to prevent access, a disastrous and unnecessary addition.

25. This is the outer of the two great state-rooms and the one most used for public audiences and meetings, from the 13th century onwards. One of the major alterations in Napoleonic times was the destruction of the upper part of the keep and the building, in the two state-rooms, of great brick ceilings, one of which is shown here. The wall on the left runs right up through the centre of the keep, dividing it into two self-contained halves.

26. (*above*) These great pillars and circular arches in the ground-level storerooms carry much of the enormous weight of the stone above them. These storerooms were necessary to provide food, wine and ale for a year for the recommended garrison of 1,000 men.

27. (*right*) The great well inside the keep, an essential feature of all defence works, ensured that a beleaguered garrison could survive. The human body can survive for long periods with limited food, but only for days without water.

Maison Dieu

28. This old etching of the Maison Dieu, undated but probably of the second half of the 18th century, shows it with pitched roofs and small dormer windows. The building was originally a hospice for travellers, later became a victualling office for the Navy and is now the town hall.

29. This, a companion to the previous etching, shows the little chapel added to the hospice in July 1227 when King Henry III came to Dover to be present at its consecration.

Ordnance  Property,

THE WHOLE FREEHOLD,

SITUATE BY THE SIDE OF THE HIGH ROAD, AT THE ENTRANCE TO

DOVOR,

IN THE COUNTY OF KENT.

THE VERY VALUABLE AND EXTENSIVE

FREEHOLD PREMISES,

KNOWN AS THE

MAISON DIEU,

FOR MANY YEARS THE NAVY VICTUALLING OFFICE,

COMPRISING

THE ANCIENT TOWER AND HOSPITAL,

CONVERTED INTO

Most Substantial, Dry, and Spacious Warehouses and Offices,

COPIOUSLY SUPPLIED WITH SPRING WATER,

With large modern Additions and Alterations, including Stabling, Forge, Saw Pit, Workshops, Sheds, Cottages, &c. &c. enclosed within high Walls,

A STREAM, 24 FEET WIDE,

FLOWS THROUGH THE PREMISES,

WITH FALL,

MOST VALUABLE FOR PROPELLING A MILL OR MACHINERY,—AND ATTACHED IS

A RENT OF £40 PER ANNUM,

ALSO THE ADJOINING

CAPITAL RESIDENCE,

OCCUPIED BY THE COMMANDING ROYAL ENGINEER,

And complete for the immediate Reception of a respectable Family,

FOR SALE BY AUCTION,

IN THREE LOTS, BY

Messrs. DAVIS, Brothers,

At the Auction Mart, near the Bank, London.

On TUESDAY, MAY 20, 1834, at 12 o'Clock,

BY ORDER OF

The Principal Officers of His Majesty's Ordnance.

The whole Premises are particularly eligible

FOR A LARGE BREWERY.

30. In 1834 the Maison Dieu was no longer needed for governmental purposes and was offered for sale by auction in three separate lots. Note that the 'capital Residence', now the public library, was considered suitable for the 'immediate reception of a respectable family', and the premises for 'a large brewery'.

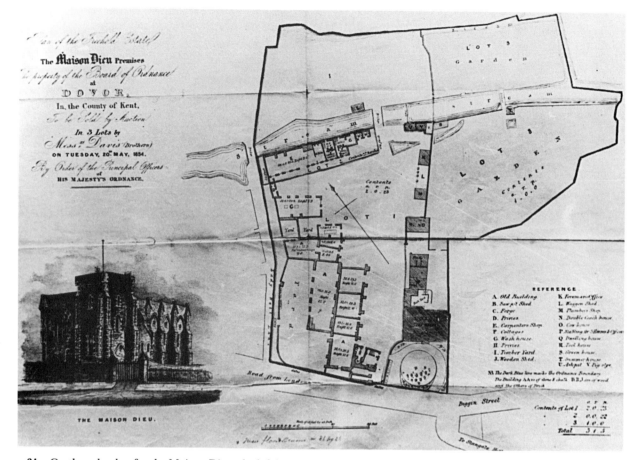

31. On the sale plan for the Maison Dieu, the left hand boundary is shown running up the middle of 'Lady Well Lane'. This marked the boundary between Dover and Charlton parish and, when the road was repaired, half the cost was borne by each authority. It is interesting to see Dover spelt as 'Dovor'.

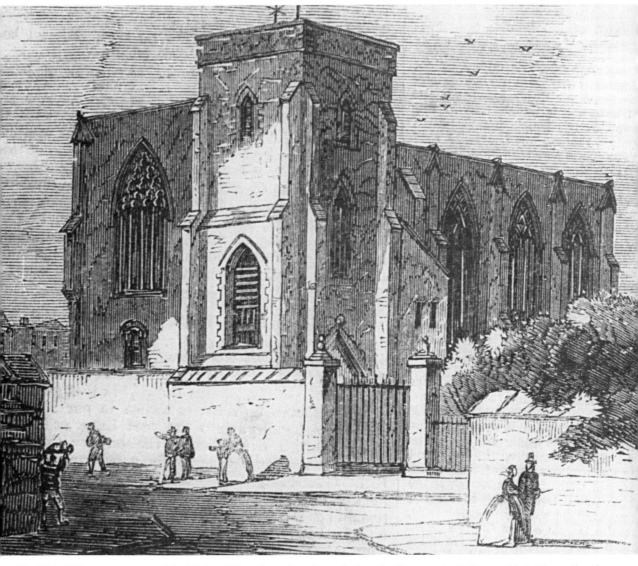

32. This 19th-century view of the Maison Dieu shows it as it was before the Connaught Hall was added. The wall and gates outside it have long been removed.

33. These arches at pavement level, which are the tops of the old entrance to the Maison Dieu, illustrate how the occupation levels of old towns rise century by century.

34. The town hall, originally the Maison Dieu, which was founded in 1203 as a hostel for travellers, a purpose it served throughout the medieval period, after which it became a victualling yard for the navy. In 1830 it was converted into a depot for the engineer services, and four years later was bought by the Dover corporation, to be restored during the 1850s and enlarged to become the town hall, its undercroft serving for some years as a prison.

Fortifications

35. Archcliffe Fort, on the north side, was a large brick-built addition to Henry VIII's original small gun platform.

36. This shows the site of the old barracks which were demolished in the 1960s, the South Front Barracks in 1965. This illustration, dated March 1987, shows the site being cleared of undergrowth and rubbish preparatory to being opened to the public. In the top left of the photograph is the Drop Redoubt.

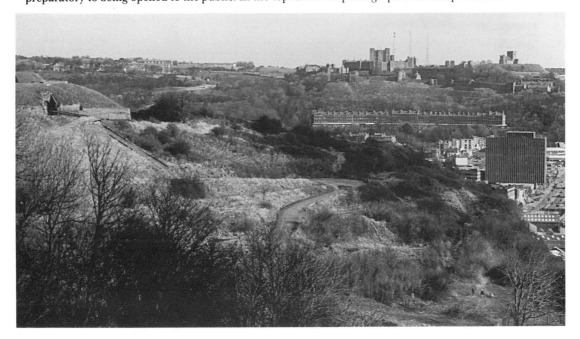

37. This fine gateway leading into the Citadel from the Archcliffe Road approach was a fine example of military engineering. It was quite inexcusably demolished a few years ago, a sad act of official vandalism.

38. The Grand Shaft Barracks on the Western Heights before their demolition, untenable in modern warfare because their exposed position would have made them a prime target from the sea.

39. (*right*) The old South Front Barracks on the Western Heights. These, shown here in decay, provided accommodation for large numbers of troops. Note the foot bridges connecting the wings.

40. (*below*) The turret on the Admiralty Pier housed two enormous guns and all their control gear which was steam powered, but when the pier was extended to complete the great harbour the guns could no longer be used. All the control gear and the engine and boiler installations have been removed, but the great guns remain, their barrel mouths being buried in concrete.

Maps and Plans

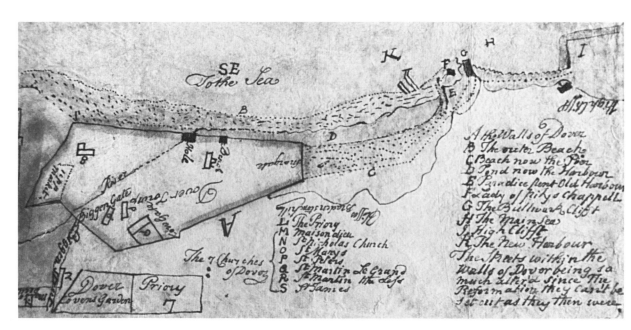

41. This ancient undated map is probably of about the mid-16th century and is drawn 'upside down' with the south at the top. The area enclosed by the firm lines to the left indicates the old town within the town walls.

42. The drawing of the town in the 1540s, taken from the larger map, showing the hills, the castle and the harbour. The many ecclesiastical buildings are clearly shown, as are sections of the old town wall, already ruinous, in the lower part of the picture. This is the oldest known illustration of the town.

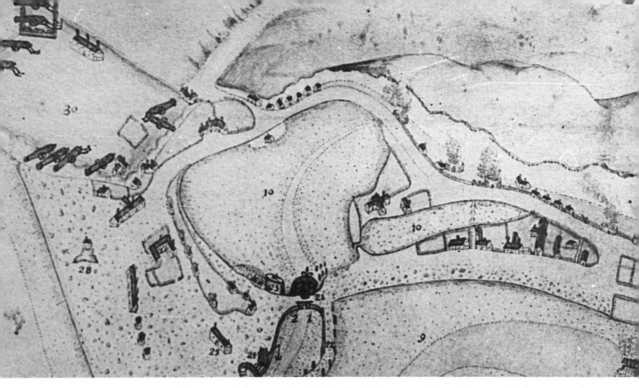

43. A section of the most valuable print of the map of 1595 labelled 'The state of Dover Haven with the new works 1595'. The five cylindrical buildings with smoke rising from them are limekilns, which gave the street its name of Limekiln Street. In the top left, numbered 30, is Archcliffe Fort, built half a century earlier.

44. This section of the 1595 map shows, on the right, the Market Square and in the middle of the square the old Market Cross. Immediately above it are the eastern remains of old St Martin le Grand, still with its three apsidal chapels. On the right is St Mary the Virgin, old St Peter's (where Lloyds Bank now stands) having by that time disappeared. At the top are surviving sections of the old town walls with battlemented tops.

Historic Buildings

45. This old priory building with its Norman style plainly shows it to be of the 1130s. It is still in good condition in spite of its chequered history.

46. The old priory entrance gate from the Folkestone road was one of the principal ways of gaining entrance to the outer or public court of the establishment. It still remains in quite good condition.

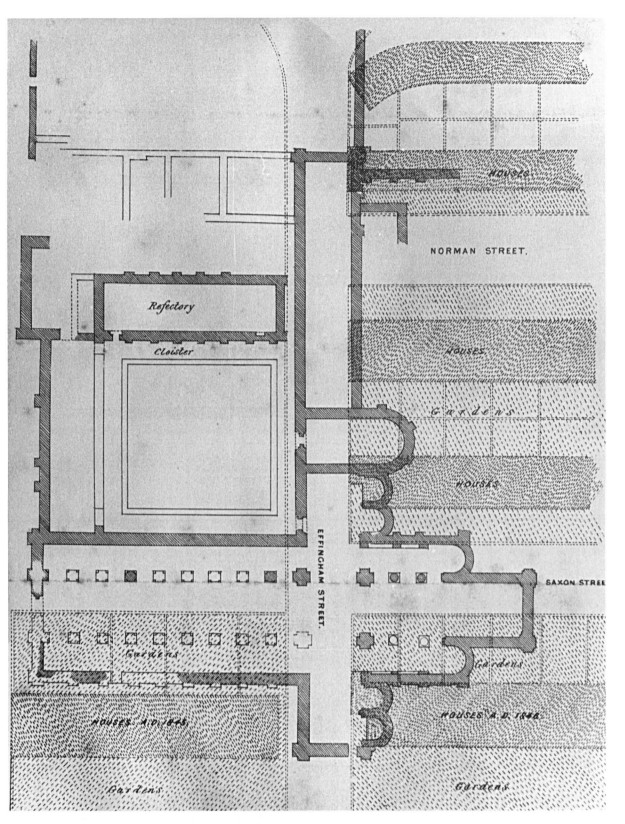

NORMAN STREET.

Refectory

Cloister

EFFINGHAM STREET.

SAXON STREET

HOUSES

HOUSES

Gardens

HOUSES

Gardens

HOUSES A.D. 1845.

Gardens

Gardens

HOUSES A.D. 1845.

Gardens

47. This plan of the private or inner court of the Priory has been silhouetted upon a plan of the modern streets which have been built on the old Priory site. The refectory survives but the magnificent great church has totally disappeared.

48. This opening in the old town wall, called 'the hole in the wall', led to the beach where the fishermen hauled **up** their boats and prepared the herring, their principal catch, for drying.

49. An old print of the old custom house, of which many must have been produced, showing the building in **about** 1806 when there was much clearance of old property in the area. It was then about 200 years old.

50. These decaying buildings lined Commercial Quay; the illustration dates from c.1840

51. Maison Dieu House, now the public library, is a fine domestic building erected in 1665 to serve as the residence of the Agent Victualler who controlled the victualling yard next door. The interior of the house has been somewhat altered, but retains a fine original staircase.

52. The original part of the Royal Victoria Hospital. This was originally built for his own occupation by Alderman
W. R. Dickenson, who owned a paper mill on part of the site occupied today by the nearby multi-storey car park. It
was bought by general subscription and opened on 1 May 1851.

53. The additional wing of the hospital, built of brick, was constructed as a permanent memorial to Queen Victoria and to Sir Richard Dickenson, who was much respected in the town and who gave generously to the hospital building fund.

54. The famous old 'Birdcage' public convenience, shown on the left hand side of this picture of people watching a procession, was demolished, to the deep regret of many Dovorians.

Churches

55. St Edmund's chapel in Priory Street has had a varied existence. Thought to have been a mortuary chapel when it **was originally consecrated** in 1253 (a burial ground once existed opposite it), it has since the 16th century been a farm **barn, a store,** a whitesmith's workshop and a meeting place before it was reconsecrated in 1968.

56. The foundations of the old Knights Templar church at Braddon, now part of the Western Heights. It had a tiny rectangular chancel and a circular nave. The walls were of flint and rubble faced with ashlar, some of which survives.

57. The old garrison church on the Western Heights was built in 1859 and was a distinctive landmark, visible from all over the area for more than a century. It stood empty and neglected from the end of the last war until it was finally demolished in 1962 to make room for domestic accommodation for the prison officers serving in the Citadel.

58. The interior of the church of St Mary the Virgin as it was before Canon Puckle rebuilt it in 1843/4. Note the fine old kingpost roof, the box pews and the candle branch.

59. The interior of St Mary the Virgin at Easter 1850 after rebuilding, a typical Victorian interior. With the exception of the reredos, the position of the font, the galleries and the arrangement of the pews, this is largely its present state.

60. (*left*) St Mary's sundial was added to the tower in 1656 during the Commonwealth. The tiny window above it is very early Norman.

61. (*below*) King Charles II, after the Restoration, ordered that his own royal arms should be hung in the most prominent part of St Mary's church where all the people would be bound to see it. After King James II had fled from the country it was pulled down and destroyed and, a few years later, those of William and Mary were hung up in their place. These are three dimensional and fairly rare, since the two monarchs did not rule jointly for long before Queen Mary died.

62. The west tower of old St Mary the Virgin in Cannon Street. The two lower stages are early Norman of c.1100, **and were** the original west tower-cum-porch of the tiny church. The upper three stages were added half a century **later and** carry on their south side a 17th-century sundial.

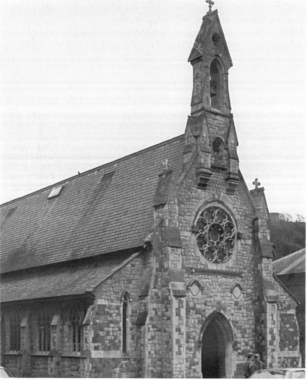

63. (*above*) Christ Church, in Folkestone Road, was consecrated in July 1844, having been built on land at the boundary of the parishes of St Mary the Virgin and Hougham. It was demolished in 1978.

64. (*left*) The Roman Catholic church in the Maison Dieu Road was opened in 1868, its congregation moving there from the old Methodist chapel in Elizabeth Street, which they had bought from the Methodists in 1835.

65. The old Methodist church in Snargate Street on the day demolition commenced in 1965. The foundation was laid in July 1834 on land leased from the Dover Harbour authority and it was opened for worship in the following October, the congregation moving from their earlier church in Elizabeth Street.

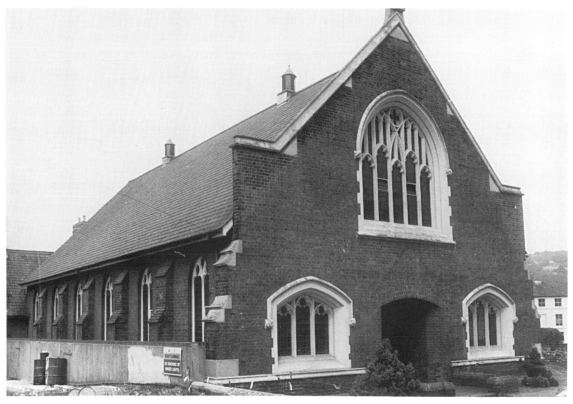

66. The Wesleyan Methodists built a hall at the town end of Folkestone Road and, soon afterwards, Wesley church which is shown here. It carries a stone, carved as follows: 'Built 1910. Bombed 1917. Rebuilt 1920. Bombed 1941. Restored 1949.' A sad record indeed. The building now serves as classrooms for Dover College.

67. The Unitarian Chapel, completed in 1820 to house one of the oldest dissenting groups in the area, tracing its formation back to 1643. It is an octagonal building with galleries and is a great treasure, being one of the few remaining almost unaltered early 19th-century preaching houses. The one alteration is that at some time in the past a large organ replaced the original pulpit, the pulpit being placed to one side, instead of remaining in the central position it undoubtedly occupied at first.

68. The Salem Baptist church in Biggin Street was built in 1840 and opened in the August of that year. It was sold and demolished in 1970, after the last service was held there on Easter Sunday, the congregation moving to a new church in the Maison Dieu Road. The site of this old building was then incorporated in the enlarged Boots the Chemist's shop next door.

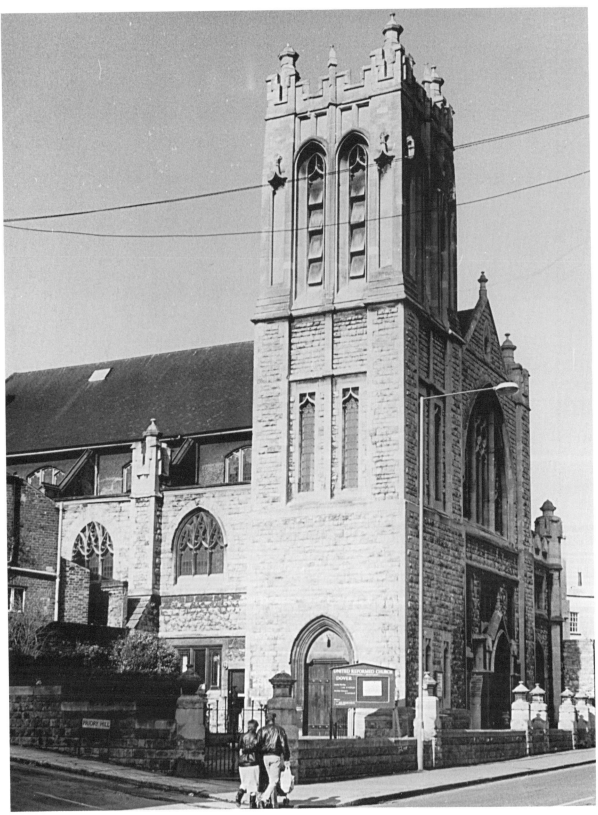

69. The United Reformed church in the High Street was built in 1903. It is a distinctive building with a large undercroft and a good tower, all of it an over-elaborate copy of the old medieval Decorated Gothic style.

Harbour and Docks

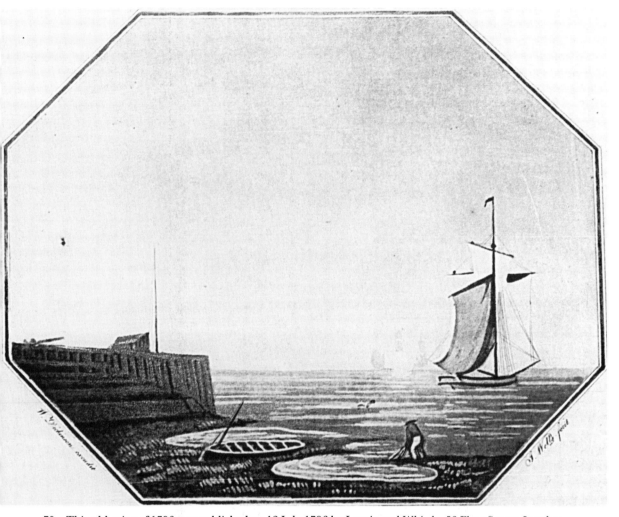

70. This old print of 1796 was published on 12 July 1796 by Laurie and Whittle, 53 Fleet Street, London.

71. A print published by the *Pictorial Times* in about the middle of the 19th century. Holy Trinity church is shown at the bottom right.

72. A lovely mid-19th-century view from the sea. In the centre are the north and south pier heads and the harbour **entrance** between them. The steamship on the right carries sails, since old sailors were often reluctant to trust the new **fangled** steam machinery.

73. These slim, lithe, paddle steamers, shown moored at the Admiralty Pier in 1880, were capable of fast passages, though of course their carrying capacity was limited.

74. In the early years of the 20th century Dover was a very popular subject for picture postcards like this, which shows the view over the Western Docks from the Heights in 1910.

75. These visual communication frames were used to give messages to ships by means of the positions of the **adjustable balls**. Now of course radio puts the harbour control centre in verbal communication with all the ships **seeking** to leave or enter, and visual signals are no longer required.

76.   These little 19th-century ships were maids of all work, ferrying passengers ashore from large Passage ships, **taking** occasional small cargoes round the coast, fishing, and even smuggling.

77.   This early steamship is shown in front of the customs and harbour house, and is typical of the early **steamers**, which were little more than large open boats with side paddles, a central boiler and steam engine, **and** provided little if any comfort or shelter for the passengers. This ship probably dates from about 1830.

78. (*above*) These later and larger paddle
steamers were more powerful, better able to
cope with rough seas, and had saloons for the
passengers. Their greater speed enabled them
to cross the channel in between one and two
hours. This photograph was taken c.1900.

79. (*right*) King George V raced this beautiful
yacht, his *Britannia*, and here she is sailing off
Dover in the Nore match.

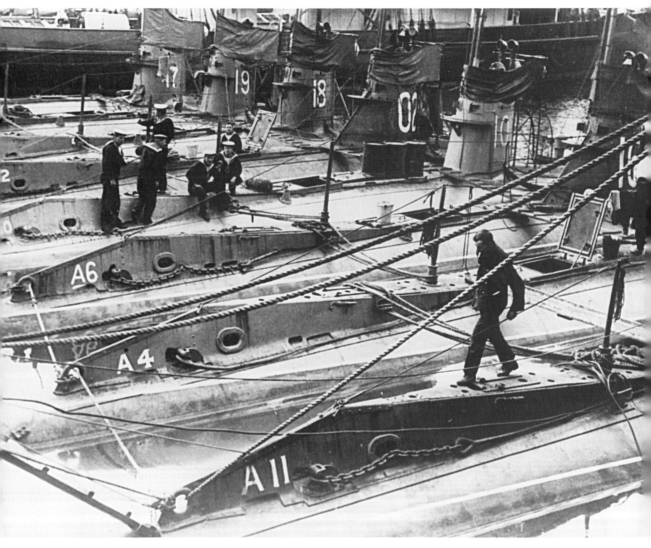

80. These submarines, in Dover harbour between the wars, were a far cry from the modern atomic-powered submarines, but they were much used and surprisingly efficient.

81. A marvellous print 'Published as the act directs by A. Hamilton Feb. 1, 1775'. In those days, long before the coming of steamships, the Passage frequently took two tides and sometimes more, so Yorrick and his wife, shown here, had to be prepared for a slow and perhaps dangerous crossing. This print was discovered among a pile of old framed pictures on a market stall.

82. This undated picture shows passengers landing at the Admiralty Pier. The north and south piers of the harbour entrance are shown in the top left-hand corner.

83. A busy scene in 1860 when the steam packet arrived. Unloading was carried out with two gangways, supervised by the important official standing on the paddle wheel cover. All baggage was man-handled.

84. An arrival at a similar spot today. The contrast is remarkable.

85. Pioneering days in the car ferry business. Here, before the advent of the drive on-drive off ferries, the work was done by means of cranes. Here a crane is loading a motor coach.

86. Wonderful views of the constant activity in the Car Ferry Docks can be obtained from the clifftop above them. Development here seems to be continuous and photographs rapidly become obsolete.

87. Peace reigns in the harbour for just one day in the year. The harbour sleeps on Christmas Day and the Passage ships lie tied up in the Western Docks.

88. The Wellington Dock, the enlarged successor to the historic Pent which was built for Dover by the command of Queen Elizabeth I. This was Dover's first artificial harbour, and without it shipping would have been reduced to small craft capable of being launched from the beach.

89. The harbour from the Western Heights, a fine vantage point. Here the effect of the harbour walls can be seen as a **strong sea** is running and yet the water inside the harbour is totally smooth.

90. This view of the breakwater is one which all who enter Dover by sea will know. Once part of the defences of the **harbour**, it is now used only by groups of sea anglers.

Promenade and Pier

91. The western end of the town, shown in the 1735 drawing, became known as the pier district. Though it later **became** somewhat run down, at this time it contained a number of substantial, well-built houses.

92. Marine Parade, drawn by George Shepherd who produced a large number of line drawings of Kent in the 1820s and 30s. Many were engraved by Adlard and published by George Virtue of Paternoster Row, London. Note the **bathing** 'engines' as they were called on the right.

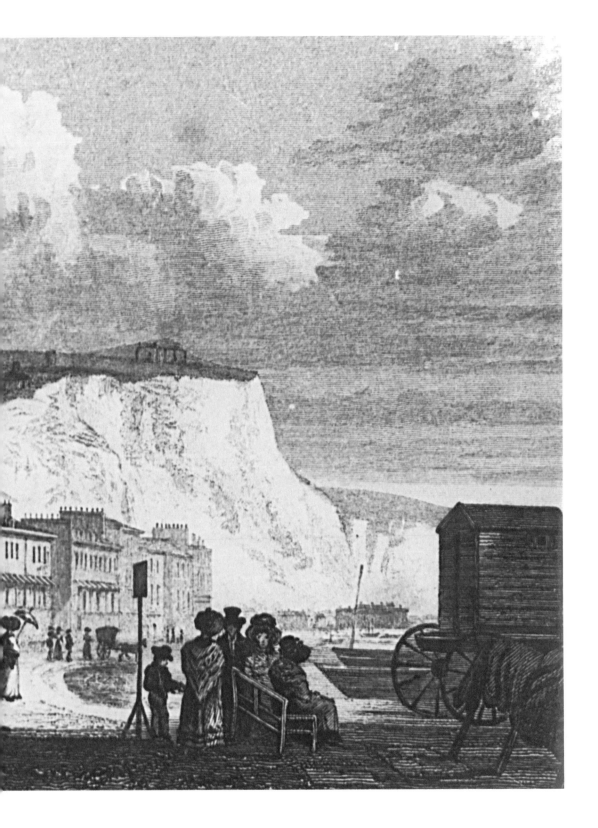

93. Here, an early 20th-century view shows the promenade built and surfaced, separating the houses from the beach. The low building on the left was Marsh's bathing establishment.

94. The promenade pier, opened in 1893, provided an additional attraction on the sea front.

95. This document, declaring that Mrs. Elizabeth Mary Cole owned two £5 shares in the Pier company, did not result in her prosperity. It was a poor investment.

96. Like most seaside piers, Dover's had accommodation for concerts at its seaward end as this view shows.

Shops, Businesses and Public Services

97. In the 19th century it was fairly common to use members of the royal family in **advertisements**. Here, tailors and outfitters have combined to advertise their shops by **adding** their names to a fine portrait of Queen Victoria.

98. The Eastes family had premises in the town and farms in the country round about. They were corn merchants, **ran farms and market gardens,** and sold their produce including hay, straw and corn, delivering it in their own carts **and wagons,** like those shown here.

99. (above) An advertisement of Walter Day Adams, showing his premises and, probably, every barrel his store held at the time. Such men were adventurous businessmen, importing quantities of goods and hoping to dispose of them in one way or another, but always taking risks from which only the cleverest, or the luckiest, eventually survived.

100. (right) Major Munn, who lived at Maxton Manor House, now demolished and the site occupied by a car sales business, invented a bar frame demountable bee hive, making it possible to inspect the swarm and take honey, without damaging the swarm. W. J. Pettit, himself a bee keeper, built and sold these and others of his own design from his Snargate Street workshop.

W. J. PETTITT, SOLE INVENTOR AND MANUFACTURER OF BEE HIVES.

Catalogues Gratis on application, or Post Free on receipt of Stamps.

These Hives afford every facility for the EXCHANGE OF QUEENS, the bar frames being movable. The LIGURIAN QUEENS are easily introduced, and to all who are interested in the collection of HONEY and WAX, PETTITT'S BEE HIVES are invaluable.

MAJOR MUNN'S BAR FRAME HIVE.
MANUFACTORY—151, SNARGATE STREET, DOVER.

101. Ingram Newman specialised in shell fish, and his shop was patronised not only by Dovorians but by many from further afield. Such specialised businesses are now becoming rare.

SOUTER MACKENZIE AND CO.,

Manufacturers of
The "CRYSTAL"
Mineral Waters,
ARMY & NAVY CONTRACTORS.

The water used is carefully filtered through solid carbon, and no cheap ingredients are employed in the manufacture of any of the

"CRYSTAL" WATERS.

Dover Works—
BLENHEIM SQUARE.   Telephone No. 213.

" **Crystal** " Soda Water, guaranteed to contain the Alkali.

" **Crystal** " Seltzer Water, an exact representation of the Natural Spring in Nassau, a nice mellow beverage.

" **Crystal** " Potass Water, useful in all Affections of the Kidneys.

Deal Works—
147½, HIGH STREET.   Telephone No. 1y4.

Folkestone Works—
FOORD ROAD.   Telephone No. 24.

" **Crystal** " Lithia Water, a specific for Gout and Rheumatism.

" **Crystal** " Lemonade, prepared from the Fruit.

" **Crystal** " Vinestal, Registered, the new Tonic, see *The Lancet,* July 7, 1894, &c.,   &c.,   &c.

Works - DOVER, FOLKESTONE & DEAL.   Sole Agents for Kops Ale & Stout.

102. (*above*) This firm, known locally as 'the Crystal', had several works in the area, but the principal one, shown top left, was in Blenheim Square in the Pier District.

103. (*left*) This old building in Bench Street was once St Mary's parsonage but when Canon Puckle became vicar in 1842 he thought it an inappropriate location so he moved elsewhere in the town. Having been Messrs. Lukey's principal shop for many years, it is now occupied by another firm of wine merchants.

104. The corner shop opposite the G.P.O., once occupied by the London Outfitters, later housed Woolworths, who extended their shop to include it. Now they too are gone, and the premises have been taken over by a bookshop and other businesses, leaving only George Lock as an old occupier in this block.

105. The end of the old threepenny and sixpenny store is shown as the Woolworth sign is being removed from its Worthington Street frontage in July 1984.

106.   The low corner building in the Market Square was originally planned to be of the same height and style **as the remainder** of the block of which it is a part, but a tiny window in the gable end of the old inn next door **prevented it,** the owners of the inn claiming 'Ancient Lights'. When the inn was rebuilt some years ago, care **was taken** to preserve the tiny window.

107.   A view which many Dovorians will remember with nostalgia. The restaurant above Igglesden and Graves's bakers' shop where tea was always a very special treat.

108. One of the very old parts of the Market Square is Igglesden's Corner, where the restaurant and bakery operated for so many years. The steps of the shop were reputed to have been those on which David Copperfield sat when he was searching for Betsy Trotwood. The premises now serve as a bookshop and stationers.

109. (*above*) This view of the Connaught Park waterworks, with smoke issuing from the chimney, was taken when it was steam powered. Now electricity is used and the chimney has been demolished.

110. (*left*) One of the matched pair of triple-expansion vertical steam engines, the last of their kind and the only matched pair in the world, pumped water up to the reservoirs at the Connaught Park waterworks from the Second World War until the Folkestone Water Company took over the undertaking, and sold one of these fine engines, to the great regret of Dover people.

111. (*above left*) This was one of the Cornish-type boilers which supplied steam for the great engines.

112. (*above right*) The Dover engines pumped water from deep wells, of which this is one, sunk into the chalk.

113. (*below*) The old Crossley oil engine which once supplied power to the pumps in the sewage system. It was of the **single-cylinder horizontal type.**

Inns and Hotels

114. The old *City of Antwerp Hotel* stood at the junction of Canon Street with the Market Square. It was much patronised by the town councillors who used to meet in the old draughty Guildhall in the Square and then promptly adjourn their meetings to the 'snug' of the *Antwerp*, where many important decisions concerning the town were made.

HÔTEL BURLINGTON, DOVER.

Tariff of Charges.

ARRIVALS.

APARTMENTS.

		PER DIEM.	
		s.	d.
Single Bed Rooms - - - -	from	3	6
Double Bed Rooms - - - -	from	6	0
Sitting Room and Bed Room (communicating)	from	20	0
Sitting Room, Bed, Dressing and Bath Room (en suite) - - - - - -	from	25	0

Larger Suites with extra Bed Rooms.

N.B.--All Suites of Rooms and a large number of Bed Rooms face directly south, with grand sea view.

Attendance, per person, per day, 1/6.

BATHS.

	s.	d.
Sea Water Bath in Bath Room - - - -	2	0
Hot or Cold Bath in Bath Room - - -	1	0
Hip Bath in Bed Room - - - -	0	6

A Hairdresser attends at the Hotel daily between the hours of 8 a.m. and 10 a.m.

No charge for Electric Light in Sitting or Bed Rooms.

115. The charges for the *Burlington Hotel* make one realise the extent of inflation over the years.

116. An external view of the *Burlington Hotel* when it was at its zenith. Facing the sea, it was one of the finest hotels in south-east England at that time.

117. The hotel lounge elegantly, if fussily, furnished in the fashion of the day.

118. (*above*) The shell of a once-great hotel, the
Burlington.

119. (*right*) More of the ruins of the *Burlington Hotel*,
one of the town's finest, and the mecca of many a
cross-channel traveller.

120. (*above*) The old *Cause is Altered* which stood in Queen Street is one of Dover's ancient inns, its original name until the end of the 18th century being *The Black Horse*. The plaque shown on the wall indicates the position of the old Cow Gate in the town wall. The inn was demolished in the 1970s when the area was cleared for redevelopment.

121. (*left*) The *Hotel de France* was demolished in the 1970s since it stood in the way of the new roundabout built at the junction of Snargate Street. It had a café, called 'The Café de Paris', a rendezvous much loved by Dovorians.

122. (*above*) The old *Prince Regent* closed its doors in 1986.
Here it is shown next to the façade of the old Market Hall
built in 1846 on the site of the earlier town gaol.

123. (*right*) The *Sir John Falstaff*, a splendid inn in
Ladywell, next to the fire station. It has a fine front of
glazed bricks and tiles and an exceptional hanging sign.

124. (*left*) The *Dover Stage*, named to commemorate the stage coach days when the horse-drawn stage coaches ran in numbers daily on the turnpike roads linking London with the Dover cross-channel ships. The building was completed in 1957, its six storeys supported upon concrete pillars, and it contrasts favourably with Burlington House, a most depressingly-ugly 12-storey office block nearby.

125. (*below*) The *White Cliffs Hotel* at the centre of Waterloo Crescent on the sea front, the principal hotel in the town, and one well known to generations of cross-channel travellers. Its windows overlook the busy harbour.

Transport

126. The turnpike gate near the castle was on the Dover-Deal-Sandwich tollroad, completed in 1797. It shows a horseman paying his dues to the tollgate keeper, who lived in the house to the right of the gate.

127. The Folkestone road and Elms Vale Road junction was the original site of the horse trough and the place was
known by that name. Here stood a turnpike gate on the Folkestone-Dover road.

128. This picture, published in the 'Graphic' on 6 November 1880, shows experimental work being carried out
on the Channel Tunnel.

South Eastern & London, Chatham & Dover.

D·O·V·E·R & D·E·A·L R·A·I·L·W·A·Y.

PRIVATE OPENING

Tuesday 14th June, 1881.

NOT TRANSFERABLE

This ticket will be available on the 14th June by any of the trains mentioned in the Programme of Arrangements & also to the Déjeûner.

129. (*above*) This is an invitation to the opening of the **Dover** to **Deal** Railway in 1881. It is issued in the name **of the** Joint Committee of the South Eastern, and of the **London, Chatham** and Dover Railway companies.

130. (*right*) The terminus of the London, Chatham **and Dover** Railway still survives. It is now almost **hidden away** in the Western Docks railway lines.

131. (*above*) Here an early train is shown using the south-eastern track at Aycliffe near the tunnel under Shakespeare Cliff.

132. (*left*) The early S.E.R. terminus on the beach. Later this, and the L.C. and D. terminus, was extended to the dockside of the Admiralty Pier.

133.   The Marine Station, a remarkable building much less appreciated than it should be. It is the last, and arguably the finest, of the great 'cathedral' type of railway termini, constructed of pre-formed iron sections hot-rivetted together. Its construction was authorised by an Act of Parliament in 1906, building was started in 1909 and was completed before the outbreak of war in 1914.

134. Arthur Baldock, a well-known figure in the steam haulage business, on his favourite and beautifully-maintained steam tractor, 'King of the Road'. Its speed was five miles per hour.

135. Steam traction engines pulled a train of several wagons and were used chiefly for heavy ballast, coal and corn.

136. This postcard of c.1910 shows the Market Square on market day. The horse-drawn wagons on the left brought in the produce from local farms. An open-top tram is shown in the middle of the picture. Note the appalling road surface.

137. Railway and tram services here, right outside Holy Trinity church, must at times have caused disturbance to the services. This photograph was taken in May 1932.

138. The tram system in Dover commenced in 1897 on two routes: from the Pier to Buckland Bridge, and from Biggin Street to Maxton. In 1905 the first route was extended to River church. This picture shows the first tram, loaded with civic dignitaries, about to start on its maiden run to River on 2 October 1905.

139. An open-top tram prepares to start from the River terminus near River church.

Demolition and Damage

140. Castle Street, a 19th-century thoroughfare, did not at first connect with the Market Square because the way was blocked by the Antwerp Stables. Eventually these were purchased and demolished and the street extended into the square. This view, from beneath the old Guildhall, shows the last load of the old stables being carted away to complete the junction.

141. The end of old Worthington Lane, when houses were demolished in 1895. The roadway was then widened and afterwards dignified by being renamed Worthington Street.

142. The last days of Beach Street when the area, part of the old Pier District, was being cleared to make a lorry park.

143. The pile of masonry at the rear of old Beach Street as the clearance nears its end in December 1975.

144. (*right*) These old houses in Albany Place were pronounced beyond economic repair, always a sad fate for places which have been home to many people in the past.

145. (*below*) The backs of the old Gorely Homes, typical of much Victorian housing for the poor. These houses were built in 1877 by Mrs Susan Gorely for 20 elderly people and overlooked the old Cowgate cemetery further up the hill.

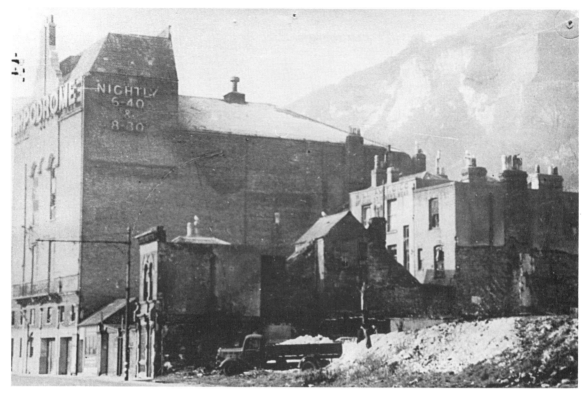

146. The town was terribly damaged during the 1939-45 war, both by aerial bombing and by shelling from **across the Channel** by long-range guns. Many of the surviving photographs are of very modest quality, having **been taken** under war conditions, as is evident in the record of the badly-damaged Hippodrome.

147. The wreckage of Chitty's flour mill at Charlton Green. This old established mill was driven both by water **wheel using** water from the River Dour, and by steam power. The mill was not rebuilt and the Dover Engineering **Works now** covers much of the site.

148. The sea front area was particularly hard hit. The only possible course of action in a case like this is, of course, complete clearance.

149. The Gateway Flats were completed in 1958 on a beautiful seafront site overlooking the busy harbour after the foundations and ruins of earlier 19th-century houses, destroyed by enemy action in the last war, had been cleared away. The six storeys contain 221 flats of varying sizes.

150. Old St James's church remained in this condition until, soon after the end of the war, the surviving part of the roof collapsed. The rubble was then cleared away and the building was left as a tidy ruin.

151. Old St James's today, a roofless ruin. The remains of the ancient tower are shown on the right, and on the extreme left is the floor of the south chapel with its own separate entrance door, in which many of the meetings of Courts of the Cinque Ports were held during the 17th, 18th, and 19th centuries.

Special Occasions

152.   A colours ceremony was always an important event in the life of regiments stationed in Dover. This shows the presentation of new colours to the 91st (Argyllshire) Highlanders in about 1860. The garrison church on the Heights is shown just to the left of centre.

153.   The Prince of Wales (later King Edward VII) laying the foundation stone of the new harbour in 1893.

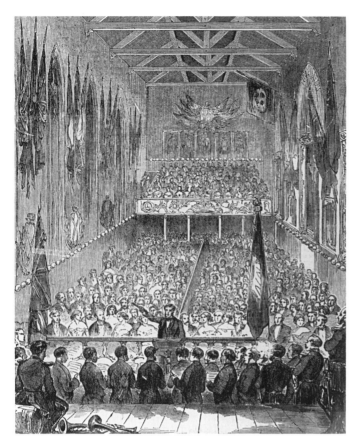

154. (*left*) Before the days of radio, television and music centres, public concerts were very popular. This shows a packed audience at a French concert in the Maison Dieu Hall in aid of the Patriotic Fund in 1855.

TOWN HALL, DOVER.

THE INAUGURATION

OF THE

Grand Orchestral Organ

PRESENTED TO THE TOWN BY

E. F. ASTLEY, Esq., M.D., J.P.

ON

Wednesday, November 5th, 1902,

At 3 and 8 o'clock.

DOORS OPEN AT 2.30 AND 7.30.

Solo Organist - - MR. H. J. TAYLOR, F.R.C.O.

(ORGANIST TO THE CORPORATION.)

This Programme admits Bearer to AFTERNOON Performance.

155. (*right*) The town hall organ, a magnificent instrument, was presented to the town by one of Dover's most distinguished citizens, Doctor Astley, in 1902. It has survived but is no longer in mint condition, though it can still be played.

156. **Great parades celebrated important events, such as royal birthdays. On these occasions the public turned out in force to enjoy the day.**

157. Visits of important people were both popular entertainment for the townsfolk and a good **advertisement**, as this picture illustrates. It adorned the Leney Brewery brochures for several years and w **accompanied** by a price list of their wares. The pyramid of barrels on the right looks extremely dangerous

158.   Regatta days always attracted great crowds. This is the 1924 event.

159.   The bandstand in the Granville Gardens was always popular in the summer, and many of the military units **stationed** in the area supplied bands to entertain the people. This photograph was taken c.1910.

160. The last church parade of the old Borough council in 1974. Those at the rear, to the extreme left, are the councillors, and those in front of them, in the trimmed robes, are the aldermen, holders of posts which became extinct at midnight on the day this photograph was taken. The annual church parade survived until 1986 when the councillors serving at that time sadly abandoned it.

161. The Lord Warden of the Cinque Ports, H.R.H. Queen Elizabeth, the Queen Mother, inspecting the naval guard of honour outside the town hall after the Court of Shepway gathering in 1979.

162. The great pageant of 1909 involved large numbers of people, and it was spoken about for years **afterwards**. This is one of the many tableaux.

163. There has been a revival of interest in pageants in recent years. In the 1986 event, two entries vividly **illustrated** the carriage of mail through the town, first by mounted post boys on horses, and then by mail **coaches**, travelling at speed on the turnpike roads and claiming priority and instant passage through the **turnpike gates**. This fine coach was loaned for the event by the Post Office.